KT-489-780

'One day you'll be battling with fog for 22 hours, looking for survivors and just as you're frozen stiff and giving up hope you spot them. Just the look on their faces when they realise they're not going to die, that's enough.'

Joe Martin

former coxswain of the Hastings lifeboat

———

© ERIC RAVILIOUS 1989 ALL RIGHT'S RESERVED DACS

COASTAL WATERS

A SMALL APPRECIATION

CREATED BY DAVID POCKNELL

Lennard Publishing
1990

Lennard Publishing
a division of Lennard Books Ltd
Musterlin House, Jordan Hill Road, Oxford OX2 8DP

British Library Cataloguing in Publication Data
is available

ISBN 1 85291 081 X

First published by Pocknell & Co in December 1989
First issued by Lennard Publishing in April 1990
Copyright © Pocknell & Co 1989

This book is copyright under the Berne Convention
No reproduction without permission
All rights reserved

Designed by Duncan Moore
Jacket illustration by Liz Pyle
Front end paper by Margaret Seaton
Back end paper by Norman Wilkinson

Printed in Great Britain by
Ebenezer Baylis & Son Ltd, Worcester
Special thanks to Jigsaw Graphics, Typesetters, Romford.
Bound by Hunter & Foulis Ltd, Edinburgh

Unless your life revolves around the middle of these islands of ours, it is hard to avoid the coast and consequently the waters surrounding us.

In East Anglia we are rarely far from our coastal waters. From time to time the otherwise friendly seas break our defences and smother some part of our shores.

Generally, however, those sometimes lapping, sometimes pounding seas provide endless pleasure for countless numbers of people.

The poets and writers whose work follows are far more adept in their words than I, so I leave it to their skill to help in expressing a small appreciation of our coastal waters.

DAVID POCKNELL
READINGS FARM
ESSEX

DAVID POCKNELL *SEA DEFENCES SOUTHWOLD*

And all the time the waves, the waves, the waves
Chase, intersect and flatten on the sand
As they have done for centuries, as they will
For centuries to come, when not a soul
Is left to picnic on the blazing rocks,
When England is not England, when mankind
Has blown himself to pieces. Still the sea,
Consolingly disastrous, will return
While the strange starfish, hugely magnified,
Waits in the jewelled basin of a pool.

SIR JOHN BETJEMAN *BESIDE THE SEASIDE*

When winds that move not its calm surface sweep
The azure sea, I love the land no more;
The smiles of the serene and tranquil deep
Tempt my unquiet mind. — But when the roar
Of Ocean's gray abyss resounds, and foam
Gathers upon the sea, and vast waves burst,
I turn from the drear aspect to the home
Of earth and its deep woods, where interspersed,
When winds blow loud, pines make sweet melody.

    Whose house is some lone bark, whose toil the sea,
Whose prey the wandering fish, an evil lot
Has chosen. — But I my languid limbs will fling
Beneath the plane, where the brook's murmuring
Moves the calm spirit, but disturbs it not.

MOSCHOS OF SYRACUSE THE OCEAN

TRANSLATED BY SHELLEY.

———

FRANCO CIRILLO

Ships that pass in the night, and speak each other in
    passing;
Only a signal shown and a distant voice in the darkness;
So on the ocean of life we pass and speak one another,
Only a look and a voice; then darkness again and
    a silence.

HENRY WADSWORTH LONGFELLOW *THE THEOLOGIAN'S TALE*

———

NORMAN WILKINSON

On the decks of many of them were parties of gay ladies and gallant yachtsmen; the gigs waiting alongside with their crews in snow-white dresses, prepared to take them on shore ... On the deck of the *Xarifa* [Earl of Wilton], that lovely schooner which attracted me more than any of the rest, the men were standing in picturesque groups, their red caps forming a striking contrast to the white spars and blue sea and sky.

MRS CONDY *THE ROYAL YACHT SQUADRON 1815–1985*

———

FRED TAYLOR

A more desolate region can scarce be conceived, and yet it is not without beauty. In summer, the thrift mantles the marshes with shot satin, passing through all gradations of tint from maiden's blush to lily white. Thereafter a purple glow steals over the waste, as the sea lavender bursts into flower, and simultaneously every creek and pool is royally fringed with sea aster. A little later the glass-wort, that shot up green and transparent as emerald glass in the early spring, turns to every tinge of carmine.

When all vegetation ceases to live, and goes to sleep, the marshes are alive and wakeful with countless wild fowl. At all times they are haunted with sea mews and roysten crows, in winter they teem with wild duck and grey geese. The stately heron loves to wade in the pools, occasionally the whooper swan sounds his loud trumpet, and flashes a white reflection in the still blue waters of the fleets.

S Baring-Gould *Mehalah*

———

FRED CUMING

The water is black with bathers: should the sea be rather rough the females do not venture beyond the surf, and lay themselves on their backs, waiting for the coming waves, with their bathing dresses in a most dégagée style. The waves come, and, in the majority of instances, not only cover the fair bathers, but literally carry their dresses up to their neck, so that, as far as decency is concerned, they might as well be without any dresses at all … And all this takes place in front of thousands of spectators … In fact, it is looked upon much as a scene at a play would be, as the gentlemen are there with their opera glasses … If the gentlemen come to look at the ladies bathing, it is equally the fact that ladies pay as much attention to the performances of the gentlemen.

THE OBSERVER *RAMSGATE 1856*

PETER BLAKE *SUR LA PLAGE*

Herring gulls heckling down to the harbour where the fishermen spit and prop the morning up and eye the fishy sea smooth to the sea's end as it lulls in blue. Green and gold money, tobacco, tinned salmon, hats with feathers, pots of fish-paste, warmth for the winter-to-be, weave and leap in it rich and slippery in the flash and shapes of fishes through the cold sea-streets. But with blue lazy eyes the fishermen gaze at that milkmaid whispering water with no ruck or ripple as though it blew great guns and serpents and typhooned the town.

Dylan Thomas *Under Milk Wood*

———

EDWARD BAWDEN

Why does the sea moan evermore?
    Shut out from heaven it makes its moan,
It frets against the boundary shore:
    All earth's full rivers cannot fill
    The sea, that drinking thirsteth still.

Sheer miracles of loveliness
    Lie hid in its unlooked-on bed:
Anemones, salt, passionless,
    Blow flower-like—just enough alive
    To blow and multiply and thrive.

Shells quaint with curve or spot or spike,
    Encrusted live things argus-eyed,
All fair alike yet all unlike,
    Are born without a pang, and die
    Without a pang, and so pass by.

CHRISTINA ROSSETTI *BY THE SEA*

COASTAL WATERS

TONY EVANS

You can start this very evening if you choose,
And take the Western Ocean in the stride
Of seventy thousand horses and some screws.
The boat express is waiting your command!
You will find the *Mauretania* at the quay,
Till her captain turns the lever 'neath his hand,
And the monstrous nine-decked city goes to sea.

RUDYARD KIPLING *THE SECRET OF THE MACHINES*

NORMAN WILKINSON

The motion of the ship was extravagant. Her lurches had an appalling helplessness; she pitched as if taking a header into a void, and seemed to find a wall to hit every time. When she rolled she fell on her side headlong, and she would be righted back by such a demolishing blow that Jukes felt her reeling as a clubbed man reels before he collapses. The gale howled and scuffled about gigantically in the darkness, as though the entire world were one black gully. At certain moments the air streamed against the ship as if sucked through a tunnel with a concentrated solid force of impact that seemed to lift her clean out of the water and keep her up for an instant with only a quiver running through her from end to end. And then she would begin her tumbling again as if dropped back into a boiling cauldron.

JOSEPH CONRAD *TYPHOON*

———

LEONARD ROSOMAN *MAN BLOWN IN THE WIND*

When tides were neap, and in the sultry day,
Through the tall bounding mudbanks made their way,
Which on each side rose swelling, and below
The dark warm flood ran silently and slow.

GEORGE CRABBE *PETER GRIMES*

EDWARD SEAGO

They say who saw one sea-corpse cold
He was all of lovely manly mould,
    Every inch a tar,
Of the best we boast our sailors are.

Look, foot to forelock, how all things suit! he
Is strung by duty, is strained to beauty,
    And brown-as-dawning-skinned
With brine and shine and whirling wind.

O his nimble finger, his gnarled grip!
League, leagues of seamanship
    Slumber in these forsaken
Bones, this sinew, and will not waken.

GERARD MANLEY HOPKINS *SEA SEQUEL*.

———

Beached Coaster Izmir

SIR HUGH CASSON *BEACHED COASTER*

We tore the iron from the mountain's hold,
By blasting fires we smithied it to steel;
Out of the shapeless stone we learned to mould
The sweeping bow, the rectilinear keel;
We hewed the pine to plank, we split the fir,
We pulled the myriad flax to fashion her.

Out of a million lives our knowledge came,
A million subtle craftsmen forged the means;
Steam was our handmaid, and our servant flame,
Water our strength, all bowed to our machines.
Out of the rock, the tree, the springing herb,
We built this wandering beauty so superb.

JOHN MASEFIELD *THE SHIP*

———

FRANK H MASON

I must go down to the sea again, to the lonely sea and the sky,
And all I ask is a tall ship and a star to steer her by,
And the wheel's kick and the wind's song and the white
        sail's shaking,
And a grey mist on the sea's face and a grey dawn breaking.

I must down to the seas again, for the call of the running tide
Is a wild call and a clear call that may not be denied;
And all I ask is a windy day with the white clouds flying,
And the flung spray and the blown spume, and the
        sea-gulls crying.

I must down to the seas again, to the vagrant gypsy life,
To the gull's way and the whale's way where the wind's
        like a whetted knife;
And all I ask is a merry yarn from a laughing fellow-rover,
And quiet sleep and a sweet dream when the long trick's over.

JOHN MASEFIELD *SEA-FEVER*

———

R ALEXANDER

O the opal and the sapphire of that wandering
        western sea,
And the woman riding high above with bright hair
        flapping free –
The woman whom I loved so, and who loyally loved me.

THOMAS HARDY *BEENY CLIFF*

———

SPENCER PRYSE

Here are our thoughts, voyagers' thoughts,
Here not the land, firm land, alone appears, may then by
       them be said,
The sky o'erarches here, we feel the undulating deck
       beneath our feet,
We feel the long pulsation, ebb and flow of endless
       motion,
The tones of unseen mystery, the vague and vast
       suggestions of the briny world, the liquid-flowing
       syllables,
The perfume, the faint creaking of the cordage,
       the melancholy rhythm,
The boundless vista and the horizon far and dim are all here,
And this is ocean's poem.

WALT WHITMAN *In Cabin'd Ships at Sea.*

———

A J JANSEN

In the days before the high tide
   Swept away the towers of sand
Built with so much labour
   By the children of the land,

Pale, upon the pallid beaches,
   Thirsting, on the thirsty sands,
Ever cried I to the Distance,
   Ever seaward spread my hands.

See, they come, they come, the ripples,
   Singing, singing fast and low,
Meet the longing of the sea-shores,
   Clasp them, kiss them once, and go.

D M DOLBEN *A Sea Song*

———

COASTAL WATERS

Anthony Eyton

———

Break, break, break,
On thy cold grey stones, O Sea!
And I would that my tongue could utter
The thoughts that arise in me.

O well for the fisherman's boy,
That he shouts with his sister at play!
O well for the sailor lad,
That he sings in his boat on the bay!

And the stately ships go on
To the haven under the hill;
But O for the touch of a vanished hand,
And the sound of a voice that is still!

Break, break, break,
At the foot of thy crags, O Sea!
But the tender grace of a day that is dead
Will never come back to me.

LORD ALFRED TENNYSON *"BREAK, BREAK, BREAK"*

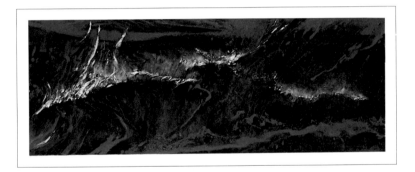

ANTHONY WHISHAW

We would like to thank all the generous contributors to this book.

Permissions have been received from the following publishers and
authors' representatives and we are indebted to them for
their promptness.

'The Ship' and 'Sea Fever', by John Masefield reproduced by permission
of The Society of Authors as the literary representatives of the estate of
John Masefield.

Extract from 'Under Milk Wood' and 'We Lying by Sea', by Dylan
Thomas reproduced by permission of the Trustees for Copyrights of
Dylan Thomas, and J.M. Dent & Son, Publishers.

Extract from 'Beside The Seaside', by Sir John Betjeman reproduced by
kind permission of John Murray (Publishers) Ltd.

We apologise to those people whom we have been unable to trace for
permission before going to print.